IMAGES OF
THE BEATLES

IMAGES OF
THE BEATLES

TIM HILL

Photographs by the

Daily Mail

p

ACKNOWLEDGEMENTS

The photographs in this book are from the archives of the *Daily Mail*.
Particular thanks to Steve Torrington, Dave Sheppard,
Brian Jackson, Alan Pinnock, Richard Jones and all the staff.

Thanks also to
Peter Wright, Trevor Bunting, Simon Taylor and Cliff Salter.
Design by John Dunne and Judy Linard.

Contents

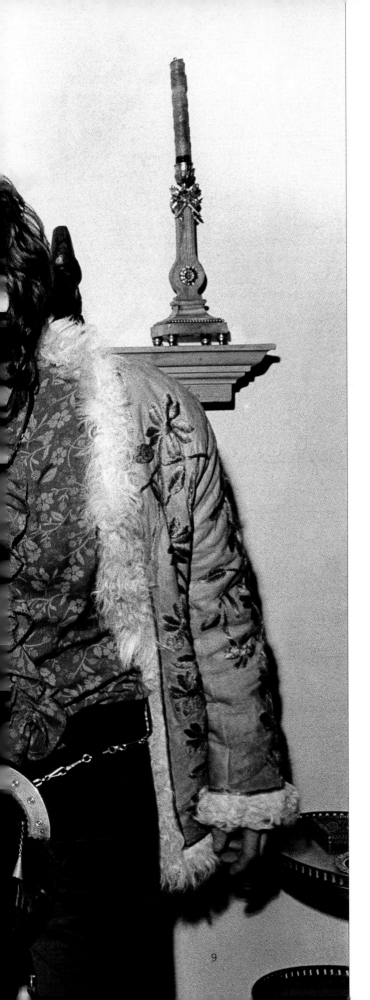

Introduction

The Beatles were one of the greatest success stories of the 1960s. Four hugely talented young men formed a group that rapidly brought pop stardom and international acclaim. Wherever they went, thousands of fans flocked in adoration; at concerts the hysteria and screams were so loud, nobody could actually hear them playing. They were to produce a unique quality of music that would prove to be timeless and respected for generations to come. After mastering the three-minute, three-chord, sad-glad pop song, they then moved on to perform increasingly innovative and sophisticated pieces that continued to hold the world's attention and admiration.

After building up a cult following at the Cavern Club in Liverpool, they released 'From Me To You', their first No.1, in April 1963. By the close of that year they had enjoyed eighteen weeks at No.1 and 'Beatlemania' had entered the English language. Their first album *Please Please Me* had reached No.1 in May of the same year and did not move until it was replaced by their second, *With the Beatles*, seven months later.

With every new release Beatles' music increased in range and complexity. *Rubber Soul* was a giant leap forward, *Revolver* was hailed as a masterpiece. *Sgt. Pepper*, widely acclaimed to be the greatest-ever rock album, was released in 1967 and saw the four scale further creative heights; their musical talents continued to develop and their fans followed them. Lennon and McCartney were beginning to be mentioned in the same breath as Schubert and Beethoven.

Their last concert was held in August 1966 in Candlestick Park, San Francisco and by 1968, cracks were beginning to show in the harmony of the band. John and Yoko Ono were totally inseparable and each of the four began to work independently. Their last public performance was in January 1969 when they held a 40-minute set on the roof of the Apple building in Savile Row, London. The highlight of this was 'Get Back' which was to be their sixteenth British No.1. The seventeenth and last was 'The Ballad of John and Yoko' which only featured Lennon and McCartney. By May 1970 when the album and film *Let It Be* were released, the band was no longer together. McCartney was the first to leave but only by a whisker. There followed months of wrangling and resentment, particularly when the business affairs needed to be wound up. Importantly however, they were all to continue to produce outstanding and influential music long after they separated.

During the decade the 'Fab Four' had produced music that was unique and timeless. The quality of their work is still held with respect and awe today. They left a legacy which will still be treasured by generations to come and, unlike many other bands, produced a bubble that is unlikely ever to burst.

Images of the Beatles is a collection of fabulous photographs from the archives of the *Daily Mail* taken by Associated Newspapers' photographers. Along with the detailed commentary, the pictures provide an insight into how four young men influenced an entire generation and beyond.

Chapter One
1960-1963

TELEVISION DEBUT

Above: 17 October, 1962. Between lunchtime and evening slots at the Cavern Club the Beatles make their TV debut on Granada's *People and Places*, performing 'Some Other Guy' and 'Love Me Do'. George Martin was unimpressed by the latter and wanted the group to record a Mitch Murray song, 'How Do You Do It?' as their debut single. 'Love Me Do' reached number 17 in the UK, while Gerry and the Pacemakers took Murray's song to number one in April the following year. Martin was vindicated, yet he showed great foresight in allowing the group to choose a self-penned number for their first release.

Opposite: The boys take a break from a hectic recording and performing schedule. The moderate success of 'Love Me Do' meant that success beyond the north-west region was far from guaranteed. In November 1962 an audition for BBC Television received a lukewarm reception. 1963 would be the breakthrough year.

FAMILY ACT

Above: Unlike a lot of pop acts at the time the Beatles appealed to mums and dads as well as the kids. Writer-broadcaster Godfrey Winn shows he is in touch with pop music's hottest property by posing with the Fab Four. It is said that the humming of Beatles' tunes was regularly heard in the royal residences, Princess Margaret being a particular fan.

Opposite: By the end of 1963 the Beatles needed much more than fancy headgear to fool their legions of fans. On 3 August that year they played the Cavern Club for the last time after more than 300 appearances. The group was about to enter pop music's stratosphere.

YEAH, YEAH, YEAH!

Left: In 1963 the Beatles had four hit singles, including three number ones, and two hugely successful albums. Many tried to analyse their style, and George Martin himself raised the occasional eyebrow when John and Paul defied convention. Their songwriting was largely instinctive; neither had any substantial knowledge of music theory.

Opposite: Clowning with Morecambe and Wise during rehearsals for the comedy duo's show, recorded in December 1963 and aired the following April. The boys donned boaters and striped jackets and crooned 'Moonlight Bay' for a musical collaboration sketch. Eric arrived in full Beatles regalia screaming, 'Yeah, yeah, yeah!'

WITH THE BEATLES

Above: John signing copies of *With The Beatles*. The group's second album replaced their first, *Please Please Me*, at the top of the album charts on 7 December, 1963. EMI didn't like the famous black-and-white cover photograph by Robert Freeman, thinking it downbeat and depressing. They were much happier with the fact that it earned silver disc status even before its release, with advance orders of 300,000.

Opposite: In costume for a sketch in *The Beatles Christmas Show*, which ran at the Astoria Cinema, Finsbury Park, from 24 December, 1963 until 11 January, 1964. The show featured other artists from Brian Epstein's stable including Cilla Black and Billy J. Kramer, both of whom had hits with Lennon-McCartney compositions. The 100,000 who managed to get tickets for the show had come to see just one act, however.

MARKETING THE FAB FOUR

Opposite: Three weeks after their phenomenally successful appearance on *Sunday Night at the London Palladium,* the Beatles take the stage at the Prince of Wales Theatre for the Royal Command Performance. They were not top of the bill this time but undoubtedly stole the show with their four-number set. John introduced their final song, 'Twist And Shout', with his celebrated remark: 'Will those in the cheaper seats clap your hands; the rest of you can just rattle your jewellery.' The Queen Mother, like the rest of the audience, loved it. After the show she asked them where they were playing next. On receiving the answer 'Slough', the Queen Mother replied, 'Oh, that's near us.'

Above: Inevitably the Beatles were trend-setters as well as musicians, and their hairstyle and clothes were slavishly copied. Apart from making some poor deals for the group's musical output, Brian Epstein badly misjudged the merchandising market. The rights were sold for a pittance, costing the group millions.

I WANNA BE YOUR MAN

Above: A lucky fan gets a personalised autograph from George. When the worldwide Beatles phenomenon took off signed photographs were often penned by members of their entourage.

Opposite: Ringo in party mode. It was barely a year since he was replaced by a session drummer for some of the 'Love Me Do' takes but he was now well established and hugely popular with the fans. John and Paul made a point of giving him the occasional lead vocal. On *With The Beatles* it was 'I Wanna Be Your Man', which they subsequently offered to the Rolling Stones.

I WANT TO HOLD YOUR HAND

Right: Ringo gives the ailing corduroy industry a major shot in the arm as the Beatles arrive in Huddersfield for a show. On the music front, the pre-release sales of 'I Want To Hold Your Hand' guaranteed that it would reach number one. George Martin again tried to convince Capitol Records that they should promote the Beatles in America. Once again the reply came back that they wouldn't make it across the Atlantic.

Opposite: George enjoying himself at a party following a gig at the Granada Cinema, East Ham. On the same day, 9 November, 1963, George signed a separate five-year contract with Northern Songs. At the time he was simply glad to get a publishing deal. He was dismissive of 'Don't Bother Me', which became the first Harrison song to be recorded by the group when it featured on *With The Beatles*. As the volume and quality of his output increased he realised that in the contract he had signed away ownership of his music.

THE BEATLES CHRISTMAS SHOW

Opposite: 26 December, 1963. Ringo at the controls of the Viking aircraft chartered by Brian Epstein to take the group and other northern-based performers in *The Beatles Christmas Show* back to London following a short festive break. The cost was £400 but that was a drop in the ocean to Epstein, who was making £2,000 a week from his Beatles contract alone.

Above: The presence of a Beatle causes a stir at a West End theatre. Accompanying Paul is his future fiancée, Jane Asher, whom he met in April 1963 following a show at the Royal Albert Hall.

Chapter Two
1964

BEATLES IN PARIS

Right: John and George en route to France, where the Beatles did 20 shows in 18 days at the Paris Olympia early in 1964. They shared the bill with American singer Trini Lopez and French chanteuse Sylvie Vartan, both of whom were received more warmly. During their stay they recorded 'She Loves You' and 'I Want To Hold Your Hand' in German in order to boost sales in that country. It was the only time the group recorded in a foreign language – and totally unnecessary.

Opposite: In Paris the Beatles attracted mild curiosity rather than the usual screaming mobs. The lukewarm reception by French fans was in marked contrast to their second appearance on *Sunday Night at the London Palladium* just before they crossed the Channel. They topped the bill again, this time for a fee of £1,000, four times the amount they received for their first appearance three months earlier.

FIRST AMERICAN NUMBER ONE

Opposite: The one bright note during their unhappy spell in Paris was the news that 'I Want To Hold Your Hand' had reached number one in America. Having allowed the previous singles to be released on the Vee-Jay and Swan labels, Capitol Records finally decided to throw their weight – and some of their marketing budget – behind a Beatles single.

Right: John and Cynthia at London Airport waiting to board the plane for New York. John was extremely sceptical about their chances of succeeding in America, something no British act had managed to do. Epstein realised that exposure was the key. The fee he negotiated for the back-to-back appearances on *The Ed Sullivan Show* was a derisory $10,000. In return for the rock-bottom fee he demanded the all-important top-of-the-bill spot.

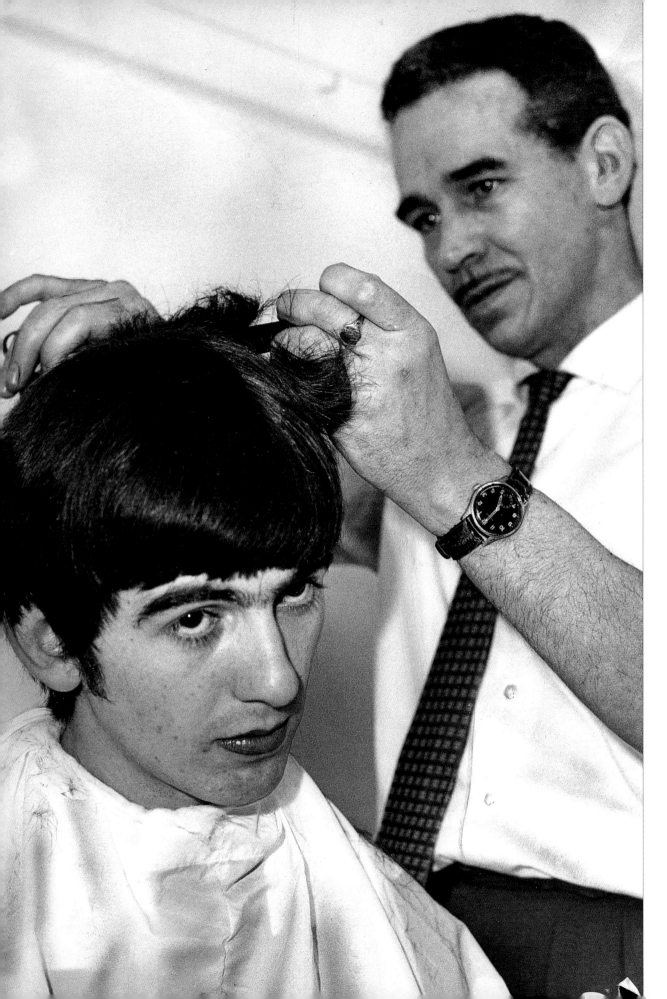

READY TO ROCK AMERICA

Opposite: George's parents, Harold and Louise Harrison, help with the packing as the Beatles prepare to crack America. Harold had wanted George to become an electrician. Louise was the music fan and she encouraged George's aspirations. It was Louise who found the £3 15s for George's first guitar, which he bought from a friend.

Left: Some of the most famous locks in showbusiness get special treatment as the boys prepare for their trans-Atlantic trip. George was the only member of the group who had been to the United States before, in 1963. He discovered that the music shops hadn't heard of them or the singles they'd released there, let alone the fans. That was all about to change.

The Beatles played three sell-out concerts during their two-week stay, one at Washington Coliseum and two at New York's Carnegie Hall. In Washington the stage was in the centre of the auditorium. The boys kept moving their equipment round – including Ringo's drums – so that all the fans got a good view of their new idols.

The Beatles' two live appearances on *The Ed Sullivan Show* both attracted record audiences of over 70 million. Reported crime levels dropped dramatically as Americans were glued to their TV sets. The following day they relaxed with a leisurely carriage ride in Central Park.

THE ED SULLIVAN SHOW

Opposite: On the first Sullivan show, aired on 9 February, 1964, the group sang three numbers at the start of the show: 'All My Loving', 'Till There Was You' and 'She Loves You'. In the second half they sang 'I Saw Her Standing There' before finishing with their Hot 100 number one, 'I Want To Hold Your Hand'. It was an accomplished performance, although the sound balance wasn't perfect. It is said that during rehearsals the sound console was marked with chalk, which was subsequently wiped off by a diligent cleaner.

Above: Rehearsing for the Sullivan show, with the inevitable phalanx of photographers. In addition to the two live performances, the Beatles taped a set to be included in the show that went out on 23 February, by which time they had returned home. A third appearance for the $10,000 fee represented excellent business for Sullivan, but it was also of incalculable importance to the group.

THEN THERE WAS MUSIC...

Opposite: Sightseeing in the capital. The Beatles' debut concert performance at Washington Coliseum on 11 February was a stunning success. The group played a 12-song set including the single releases that had bombed in America the previous year. All were now reissued and became smash hits. 'Love Me Do' went to number one, whereas in the UK it only just made it into the Top 20.

CAPITAL BEATLES

Left: Even though they were now the hottest property in the pop music world the Beatles were still just four Liverpool lads with no airs and graces. It was Epstein who liked the kudos of playing at prestigious venues such as Carnegie Hall. During a reception at the British Embassy in Washington they showed they had little time for pomp and ceremony. They were particularly unimpressed when someone snipped a lock of Ringo's hair. John stormed out after firing off a volley of expletives.

HOT SUCCESS

The Beatles left New York for Miami on Thursday 13 February, 1964, three days before their second appearance on *The Ed Sullivan Show*. Between rehearsals the boys took in the Florida sunshine and laid-back lifestyle. People were only too eager to let the Beatles borrow their yacht or use their pool. Ringo managed to prang a speedboat but the owner took it as a badge of honour that his vessel had been damaged by a Beatle.

CAN'T BUY ME LOVE

Frolicking in the surf on Miami beach. Unlike at home, Ringo was a star attraction for American fans. On the second Sullivan show they again played 'She Loves You', which eventually replaced 'I Want To Hold Your Hand' at the top of the Billboard chart on 21 March. By then there were two million advance orders for the new single, 'Can't Buy Me Love'. Unsurprisingly that went straight to number one. On 4 April, 1964 the Beatles occupied the top five places in the American Billboard singles chart, a feat unmatched either before or since.

CHAMPIONS OF AMERICA

Opposite: Cassius Clay was just a contender when he met the world's undisputed top group on 18 February, 1964. A few days later Clay became number one in his field too, after beating champion Sonny Liston. Like most people the Beatles thought Liston would win and agreed to the photo-shoot with the brash young challenger only after the champion declined.

Right: Fan club secretary Bettina Rose helps George with the 52 sacks of mail which arrive on his 21st birthday, 25 February, 1964. Jelly babies were a popular present, following reports that George had a weakness for them. Louise Harrison sent a request to the BBC to play the Miracles' song 'Shop Around' to celebrate her son's big day. It was played on the Light Programme on Saturday 22 February, the day the Beatles returned from America.

A HARD DAY'S NIGHT

Above: Paul and Ringo filming the nightclub scenes for *A Hard Day's Night* at Les Ambassadeurs Club, London. The title of the group's first feature film came from a throwaway line by Ringo during shooting. John and Paul wrote some of the songs featured in the film in Paris, some during the trip to America. When the title of the film was settled upon they quickly came up with an idea and penned a typically catchy song to complete the soundtrack.

Opposite: 21 March, 1964. George with actress Hayley Mills at a charity performance of the film *Charade*. The distinctive chord which opened the film's title track was played by George on the 12-string Rickenbacker presented to him during the recent trip to America.

All the group enjoyed filming, apart from the early morning starts. On one occasion Ringo went on set straight from a nightclub and struggled with even the simplest lines. Atmospheric shots of him looking miserable and forlorn – with no dialogue – were used instead, requiring no acting whatsoever.

A welcome break from the busy shooting schedule. Paul and Jane Asher with dancer Lionel Blair and comedian Dickie Henderson at a party in honour of Sammy Davis Jr held at the Pickwick Club. In the film each of the Beatles was due to feature in a solo set piece. Paul's scenes ended up on the cutting-room floor.

PATTIE AND GEORGE

The make-up scenes for *A Hard Day's Night* saw Pattie Boyd running a comb through George's hair. Pattie was a model who had worked with director Richard Lester previously, on an advertisement for Smiths crisps. She and George hit it off immediately and were soon a serious item.

WORKING LIKE A DOG

Opposite: A break in filming at Twickenham Studios. United Artists were not so much interested in the film as in acquiring the rights to a lucrative Lennon-McCartney soundtrack album, which was not covered in their existing record contract. Producer Walter Shenson was prepared to offer the Beatles 25 per cent of the profits and was only too pleased when Brian Epstein demanded nothing less than 7.5 per cent. Shenson also shrewdly negotiated a deal in which the rights to the film reverted to him after 15 years.

Left: Sustenance and lubrication for John as he prepares to perform, as usual with his six-string Rickenbacker. The concert scenes for *A Hard Day's Night* were filmed at London's Scala Theatre. Union rules dictated that the audience had to be paid for the privilege of hearing the Beatles play. One of those who picked up his £3 15s fee was 13-year-old Phil Collins, who would go on to rock superstardom both with Genesis and as a solo performer.

YOU CAN'T DO THAT

19 March, 1964. Receiving the Variety Club award for Show Business Personalities of 1963 from Opposition leader Harold Wilson. Later in the day the group went into the BBC studios to record their debut appearance on the organisation's fledgling *Top of the Pops*, which had aired for the first time on 1 January that year. The Beatles sang 'Can't Buy Me Love' – which became their fifth UK number one – and also the B-side 'You Can't Do That'.

Opposite: Thumbs-up at the Variety Club awards. The Beatles were not simply a pop phenomenon but also a licence to print money. The contribution to the Exchequer in overseas earnings was huge. The four were not financially savvy at this point, more interested in artistic expression than the bottom line. 'Taxman' was still two years away and it was even longer before they got to grips with the labyrinthine deals that were done in their name.

Right: 20 March, 1964. A day after making their *Top of the Pops* debut the Beatles feature on ITV's flagship pop show *Ready, Steady, Go!* The group mimed to three songs, including 'Can't Buy Me Love'. They bemoaned the quality of the sound equipment in television studios, which often left a lot to be desired.

IN HIS OWN WRITE

Above: Walter Shenson, producer of *A Hard Day's Night*, has every reason to smile. The film became a classic of its genre and he profited handsomely. The band members received a flat fee. John takes the photo-opportunity to publicise his first book, *In His Own Write*, which was published on 23 March, 1964.

Opposite: 23 March, 1964. The Duke of Edinburgh presents the Carl-Alan Awards at the Empire Ballroom, Leicester Square. The Beatles receive two awards, Best Group of 1963 and Best Vocal Record, for 'She Loves You'.

Opposite: Filming the nightclub scenes for *A Hard Day's Night* at Les Ambassadeurs, 17 April, 1964. The Beatles had recorded the film's and album's title track the previous evening at Abbey Road. The album reached number one in the UK on 25 July and stayed there until the week before Christmas, when it was toppled by the next Beatles release.

Above: With *A Hard Day's Night* still in production the group appeared in a one-hour special, *Around The Beatles*, which aired on 6 May. In the show they performed a spoof version of *A Midsummer Night's Dream* as well as a string of their hits. They were concerned about the sound quality of live performance but had agreed not to mime to their records for the musical interludes. The issue was neatly resolved by miming to a specially recorded set. Guests on the show included Long John Baldry and PJ Proby.

Opposite: Scotland lays out the welcome mat. A day after recording *Around The Beatles* at Wembley Studios the Beatles pay a flying visit north of the border. They played the ABC Cinema, Edinburgh, on 29 April and put on two shows at the Glasgow Odeon the following day.

Above: Two lucky Scottish fans get to meet their idols. The contractual agreement which made cinemas – with their limited capacity – a regular concert venue meant that large numbers of fans who wanted to see the shows were disappointed.

SCOTLAND GOES WILD

Opposite: On stage during the two-day visit to Scotland. The heavy curtains, typical for cinemas at the time, made for a bland backdrop for a pop concert but the Beatles needed no glitz or razzmatazz to send audiences into raptures.

Above: Which way to the stage? This good-humoured banter for the cameras quickly became a serious concern. The punishing schedule meant that eventually the band would scarcely know which town they were in, let alone which theatre.

WAXING LYRICAL

Opposite: Yet another photo-call. The demand for publicity shots and interviews was as relentless as the requests for the Beatles to perform. And when they did play the performance was invariably drowned out by the screaming. The four tolerated this state of affairs – for now.

Above: Four of the most recognisable faces in the world were unveiled at Madame Tussaud's at the beginning of May. The group had spent one week short of a year at the top of the album charts when they were toppled by the Rolling Stones on 2 May. The Beatles had yet to release their two LPs for the year, though, and together these would give them another six months at number one.

After spending most of May 1964 recharging their batteries on separate holidays the Beatles reconvened for a show at the Prince of Wales Theatre, scene of their triumphant Royal Command Performance the previous November. It was also a warm-up for their forthcoming world tour. In between concert commitments the group returned to the studio to record the non-soundtrack songs for *A Hard Day's Night*.

WORLD TOUR

Tuning up for the world tour...and toasting its success. Even though 'Can't Buy Me Love' had been knocked off the number one spot in the UK chart Paul still had reason to celebrate as it was replaced by another of his compositions. 'World Without Love', which he wrote at the age of 16, was offered to Jane Asher's brother, Peter, who had a worldwide hit as one half of the duo Peter and Gordon.

FAMILY MAN

Opposite: John and Cynthia. Their son, John Charles Julian, celebrated his first birthday on 8 April, 1964. When the Beatles played *The Ed Sullivan Show* in February the screen flashed up 'Sorry girls, he's married' when John was in close-up. That didn't stop him leading the life of excess commonly associated with pop superstars.

Above: In Elizabethan costume for a sketch in *Around The Beatles*.

RINGO'S STAND-IN

Opposite: 3 June, 1964. Ringo fell victim to tonsillitis 24 hours before the start of the world tour. Jimmy Nicol, a respected session musician and member of the group the Shubdubs, is briefly catapulted into the spotlight. After a quick run-through of half a dozen numbers at EMI Studios Nicol flew to Denmark to begin his brief career as a Beatle.

Right: Paul shows off a souvenir from the second leg of the Beatles' world tour. There was a hairy moment during the stay in Holland. Fans engulfed the stage, forcing the group to beat a hasty retreat. This was a special recording for Dutch TV and they were miming the set. The music thus continued even though the band had decamped.

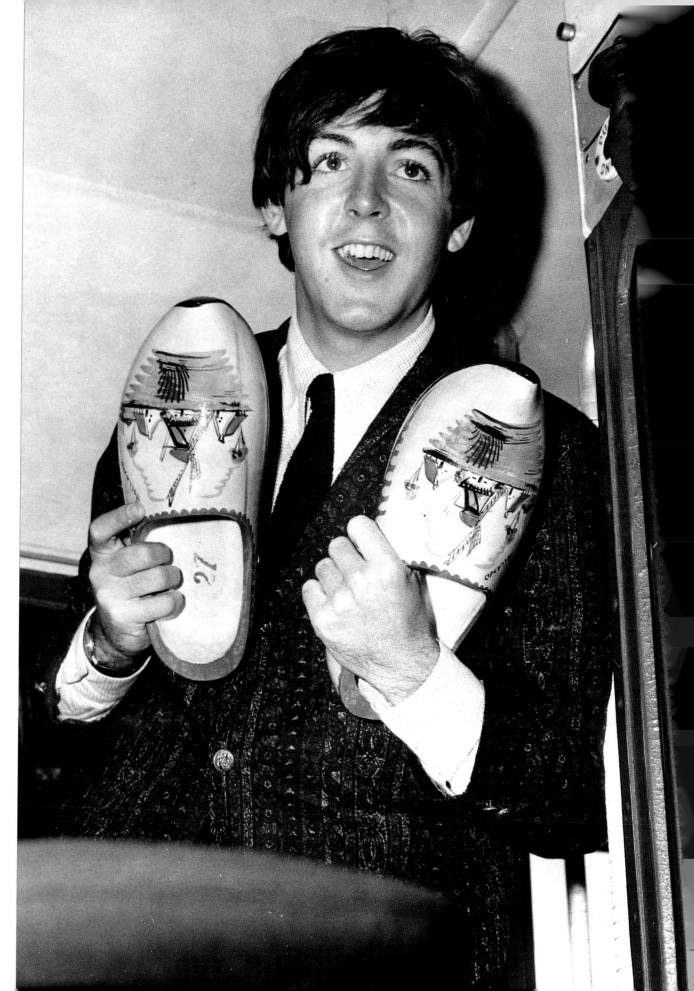

WORLD PREMIERE

Opposite: 6 July, 1964. Piccadilly Circus comes to a grinding halt as *A Hard Day's Night* receives its world première at the London Pavilion. A special northern première was held in Liverpool four days later, and the Beatles received a civic reception. Liverpudlians rolled out the red carpet to welcome home their favourite sons.

Left: From the Netherlands it was on to Hong Kong and then to Australia, where the Beatles witnessed some of the most tumultuous scenes of their touring days. Wherever they stayed they were besieged by fans. The adulation was so overwhelming and unconditional that it reminded the band of a Nazi rally. John made 'Sieg heil' gestures, a precursor to his infamous remark about the Beatles being more famous than Jesus. It was during the trip to Australia that Ringo rejoined the group and Jimmy Nicol returned to obscurity. He received £500 and a gold watch for his efforts.

Right: At the première of *A Hard Day's Night* the Beatles are introduced to Princess Margaret, who was a big fan of their music. Despite the fact that the film was shot in two months on a budget of less than £200,000, it won rave reviews, from critics as well as fans. It grossed $8 million in the first week, a huge return on United Artists' modest investment.

Opposite: On 12 July the Beatles played the Brighton Hippodrome, the first of five summer special concerts. A week later they appeared on *Blackpool Night Out*, hosted by Mike and Bernie Winters. The group performed sketches as well as music in the show, which was networked on ITV.

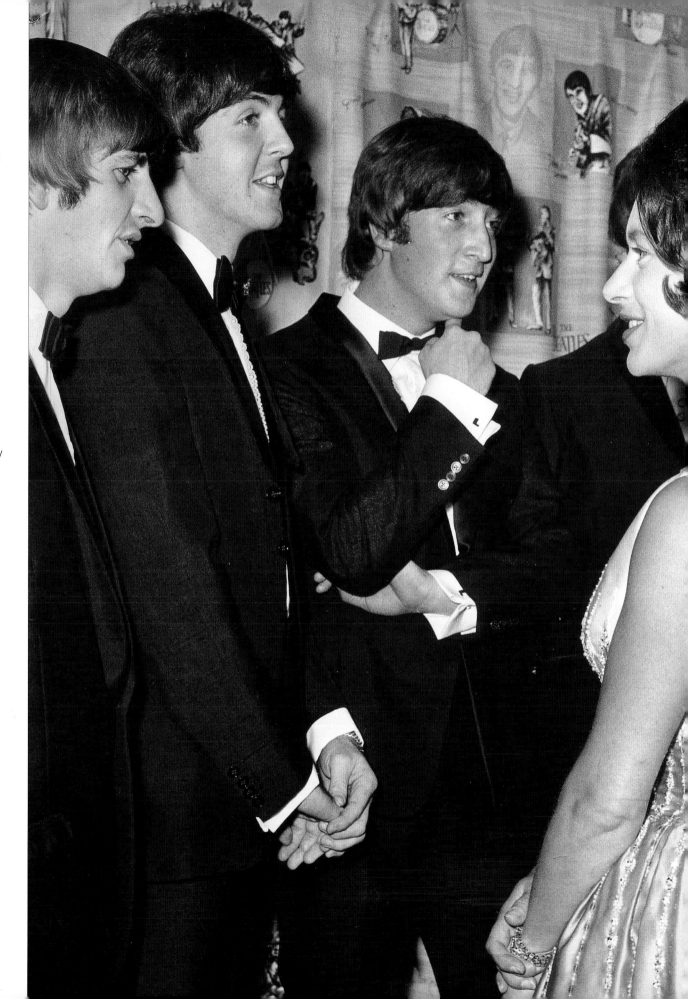

BACK STATESIDE

After several summer shows the Beatles returned to America for their first proper tour. They played 32 shows in 34 days, clocking up over 22,000 miles in the air. For their 12-song set the band typically received a fee of around $50,000. That increased dramatically when they were persuaded to play an extra gig in Kansas City, which was not on the original itinerary. Charles O. Finley, owner of the city's baseball team, wrote a cheque for $150,000 for a set lasting barely 30 minutes.

20 October, 1964. On stage in Dundee, part of the Beatles' autumn tour of Britain. It began on 9 October in Bradford, just 19 days after the end of the US tour.

BEATLES FOR SALE

Above: The touring schedule in 1964 was so relentless that it left precious little time for writing and recording. Even so the group stuck to their policy of refusing to put single releases on the albums. Despite the pressures the new LP, *Beatles For Sale*, was completed on time. On one day alone, 18 October, six of the fourteen tracks were recorded. The album was released on 4 December, replacing *A Hard Day's Night* at the top of the charts two weeks later.

Opposite: In costume for *Another Beatles Christmas Show*, which ran at Hammersmith Odeon from 24 December, 1964 until 16 January, 1965. Freddie and the Dreamers, the Yardbirds and Elkie Brooks were among the guests. The Beatles included 'I Feel Fine' in their set. The feedback sound which opened the group's seventh successive UK number one occurred accidentally when a guitar was left too close to an amplifier. The band liked the sound and decided to incorporate it into their new release.

DRIVING SUCCESS

Opposite: Twenty-four-year-old John poses outside EMI Studios in George Martin's car after passing his driving test. Success meant that the group could indulge themselves, despite some of the poor deals Epstein had negotiated. John, Ringo and George all bought houses in the Surrey stockbroker belt. Paul paid £40,000 for a house in St John's Wood and

bought an Aston Martin DB4. George Martin himself would also soon be better rewarded for his contribution to the Beatles' success. Until now the master producer had been a salaried member of the EMI staff, but in 1965 he formed his own production company and began to earn royalties from the Beatles' musical output.

TICKET TO RIDE

Above: Like all of the group John was a regular smoker. They also took amphetamines to help them cope with a demanding schedule. It was one of their musical heroes, Bob Dylan, who introduced them to marijuana. Dylan believed 'Ticket To Ride', the single released in April 1965, had a drugs message. He interpreted the line 'I can't hide' as 'I get high'.

Opposite: The Lennon-McCartney songwriting machine was in overdrive in 1965. Despite more touring commitments and another film, John and Paul still managed to write three number one singles and two chart-topping albums. Although the joint writing credit suggested an equal contribution to each song, the two usually worked independently. The collaborative process often came when one of them already had an idea for a song.

RINGO MARRIES

Opposite: Ringo became the second Beatle to marry, on 11 February, 1965. His bride was 18-year-old Maureen Cox, a former hairdresser whom he had met at the Cavern Club. The couple were married at Caxton Hall register office, London. Less than two weeks later the Beatles began shooting their second feature film.

Left: A typically rapturous send-off as the Beatles head for the Bahamas, where location filming began on 23 February. Several of the songs to be featured in the new film and on the soundtrack album had already been recorded. One of these, 'You've Got To Hide Your Love Away', featured flautist Johnnie Scott, the first time that another musician had been drafted in since session drummer Andy White replaced Ringo for some of the 'Love Me Do' takes. Scott received a £6 fee for his work.

Opposite: With Eleanor Bron, who played Ahme in the new film, *Help!* Paul liked the name Eleanor so much that he used it a year later, when he wrote 'Eleanor Rigby'. The cast also included Leo McKern, Patrick Cargill and Victor Spinetti, but the professionals couldn't salvage a project which the Beatles took so lightly.

ON LOCATION

On location in the Bahamas. The group quickly lost interest in the film, the plot of which turned on a sacred ring acquired by Ringo. Ownership of the ring endangered the life of the wearer and all manner of characters try to part Ringo from it. The group's attitude to the film wasn't helped by the fact that they smoked a lot of pot during its making. Dick Lester, again the director, had to contend with countless retakes as the band members either didn't know their lines or couldn't deliver them without giggling.

YESTERDAY

Left: Within days of competing *Help!* Paul recorded one of the most famous, and most covered, Beatles songs of all. He woke one morning with the tune of 'Yesterday' in his head and had to ask around to ascertain that he hadn't heard it somewhere. Before he put lyrics to the tune he used 'Scrambled Eggs' as a working title. 'Yesterday' was a landmark recording in that no other Beatle was involved. It also saw the use of a string quartet for the first time on a Beatles song.

Opposite: Filming in the Bahamas in February had a natural appeal. The Beatles' financial adviser had set up a tax shelter there on the group's behalf and it was thought politic for them to show their faces on the island.

6 April, 1965. Radio Caroline DJ Simon Dee presents the Beatles with a Bell Award during a break in filming at Twickenham Studios. 'Ticket to Ride', with 'Yes It Is' on the B-side, was released three days later and gave the group yet another number one on both sides of the Atlantic. John and Paul both enjoyed wordplay in their lyrics; aurally their latest hit could be interpreted as 'Ticket to Ryde', where relatives of Paul ran a public house.

Filming on a chilly Salisbury Plain in early May.
Regular soldiers on manoeuvres were on hand to
watch the Beatles perform 'I Need You', one of the
film's musical set pieces.

HELP!

Left: John, with Eleanor Bron. When the title of the film, *Help!,* was settled upon John and Paul again had to compose a song around it. In fact it was almost exclusively John's work. He was eating and drinking too much and was also conscious of his short-sightedness. The plea for help in the song lyric sprang from his poor self-image at the time.

Opposite: Ringo's vocal contribution to the new album was a cover version of a Buck Owens song, 'Act Naturally'. Originally it was going to be a Lennon-McCartney composition, 'If You've Got Trouble', which was recorded but subsequently rejected as not being up to standard. It wound up in an EMI vault, unearthed by George Martin many years later. His opinion of it would not change.

FROM MBE TO LSD

Opposite: 12 June, 1965. The announcement is made that the Beatles are to be awarded MBEs in the Queen's Birthday Honours List. The group had little time for dignitaries or official functions but decided to accept the honour. Some ex-servicemen returned their awards in protest, prompting John's acerbic comment that if people could get an award for killing people, then they deserved theirs for services to entertainment. George and Paul wore their MBEs on their *Sgt. Pepper* outfits.

Left: In late May, with *Help!* in post-production, John and Cynthia visit the Cannes Film Festival. John, along with George, readily moved on from pot to LSD in 1965. During the tour to America that year they met actor Peter Fonda, who advised caution about the drug with the words 'I know what it is to be dead' – he had once accidently shot himself. John used the line in 'She Said, She Said' on *Sgt. Pepper*, altering the speaker from masculine to feminine.

BIRTHDAY BOY

Opposite: 18 June, 1965. Paul celebrates his 23rd birthday. The following month he collected five Ivor Novello awards on the group's behalf at London's Savoy Hotel. These awards were for the group's classic sad-glad, boy-meets-girl pop songs. In 1965 the material would become much more diverse and complex.

Left: In 1965 there was increasing speculation that Paul and Jane Asher would marry. Jane's theatre work meant that the couple spent a considerable amount of time apart. She also didn't embrace the drug culture. This was the year in which the Beatles' music took a giant leap forward with the seminal *Rubber Soul* album, and drugs were a major influence. John called it the 'pot album', although they were careful not to record while under the influence.

SHEA STADIUM

Above: On 13 August, 1965 the Beatles departed for their third trip to America. Two days later they played their first, and most famous, concert at New York's Shea Stadium. The group had planned to enter the arena by helicopter but this was forbidden by the authorities. Instead they arrived in a Wells Fargo armoured truck. Vox had made special 100-watt amplifiers to cope with such venues but these still proved inadequate. It was an extraordinary visual event, if not a musical one. Two future Beatle wives, Linda Eastman and Barbara Bach, were in the 55,000-strong audience.

Opposite: 4 July, 1965. Returning from a short European tour John strikes a pose to reflect the fact that they had just played two concerts at bullring venues in Barcelona. Perhaps he was also giving a subtle plug to his new book, *A Spaniard in the Works*, which had just been published.

Above: 26 October, 1965. Buckingham Palace is besieged by fans as the Beatles arrive for the investiture ceremony. They were due to deliver a new album before the end of the year, but because of filming and touring commitments had only just returned to the studio. Not only was the brilliant *Rubber Soul* album finished by 3 December but a new single, 'Day Tripper'/ 'We Can Work It Out' – neither of which appeared on the album – was also ready for the same release date. The greater sophistication of the new material meant that recreating the sound live would have been difficult. This was of no great concern, given the group's increasing disenchantment with concert performances.

Opposite: Paul and Ringo have a smoke as they set off for the palace from Ringo's house in Montagu Square. It became part of folklore that the group smoked a joint in one of the royal toilets. George insisted that they only had a cigarette and that the story was embellished with the passage of time.

ONLY TIME WILL TELL...

Of the four it was the rebellious John who was most concerned about accepting the MBE. He eventually returned his on 25 November, 1969. In the accompanying letter he said it was 'in protest against Britain's involvement in the Nigeria-Biafra thing, against our support of America in Vietnam and against "Cold Turkey" slipping down the charts'. Brian Epstein wasn't honoured and did not attend the investiture ceremony at Buckingham Palace.

Chapter Four
1966-1967

GEORGE TIES THE KNOT

21 January, 1966. Twenty-two-year-old George marries Pattie Boyd at Epsom Register Office, with Paul doing the honours as best man. John and Ringo were holidaying in Trinidad and sent their congratulations by telegram. *Rubber Soul*, which featured two Harrison songs, was at the top of the album charts, while 'Day Tripper'/ 'We Can Work It Out' had given the group their third successive Christmas number one. Both songs were included in *Yesterday And Today*, a new album specifically for the US market. This would become a collector's item for photographer Robert Whittaker's famous 'butcher' sleeve, which was hastily withdrawn by Capitol Records and replaced with a less controversial image.

I'M LOOKING THROUGH YOU

Left: Paul strides ahead of Jane Asher as they attend a preview of her new film, *Alfie*. Jane follows on with brother Peter. 'I'm Looking Through You', written by Paul for the *Rubber Soul* album, was about the superficiality of the couple's relationship. If the love affair was cooling, album sales were not. *Rubber Soul* topped the UK chart for nine weeks between December 1965 and February 1966.

Opposite: 1 May, 1966. The Beatles play a 15-minute set at the *New Musical Express* Poll Winners Concert, held at the Empire Pool, Wembley. It was their first performance since the short British tour at the end of the previous year. That had merely confirmed their antipathy towards live gigs and their standard of musicianship began to slip as a result. They closed their set at the *NME* concert with 'I'm Down'. This would be their last live performance in their home country, and owing to a contractual dispute it was not captured on film.

A RETURN TO HAMBURG

Opposite: 23 June, 1966. The Beatles return to Germany for the first time since their final trip to Hamburg in December 1962. Although they could now afford to do everything in style, none of the group looked forward to the tour with any enthusiasm. They had just put the finishing touches to their seventh, as yet unnamed, album. *Revolver*, released on 5 August, would be proclaimed a masterpiece, yet none of the new material was included in the 11-song set for the tour.

Above: 16 June, 1966. The Beatles make their only live appearance on *Top of the Pops*. It was a coup for the show, despite the fact that they mimed to both sides of their new single – 'Paperback Writer' and 'Rain'. The double-tracking on 'Paperback Writer' made it difficult to reproduce live, a problem that would help to steer the group away from performance and towards studio work. This was also evident in John's song, 'Rain', which featured backwards guitar. He discovered the distinctive sound after running a tape from a studio session backwards by accident.

TAXING TIMES

Opposite: The six shows in Germany revealed a woeful lack of preparation, although the group knew that any flaws would always be masked by the fans' screams. For the Japanese leg of the tour they were kept as virtual prisoners at the Tokyo Hilton by over-zealous police. Things got much worse in the Philippines, where a mix-up caused them to miss a function organised by the president's wife, Imelda Marcos. The two concerts in Manila went well but news of the Beatles' 'snub' was reported on TV and there were ugly scenes at the airport when they left the country.

Right: George's 'Taxman' was the opening track on the new album, which the group also considered calling *Abracadabra*. The trenchant lyrics came from the discovery that the Beatles were paying 19s 6d in the pound to the government from their earnings. George was becoming increasingly drawn towards Indian music and culture. He had lessons from the virtuoso sitar player Ravi Shankar and planned to visit Delhi at the end of the tour to buy an instrument from one of the country's leading makers.

AN END TO TOURING

Left: Shocked by events in the Philippines, the last thing the Beatles wanted was another trip to America. The cost of pulling out would have been too great and the tour went forward on schedule. They walked into another storm as the transcript of an interview John had given to the *Evening Standard* in March was printed in an American magazine. The Bible Belt was incensed by John's comment that the Beatles were 'more popular than Jesus now', which Americans took as a statement of blasphemous arrogance. Beatles music was banned from the airwaves, and their records burned on public bonfires. John apologised and the tour went ahead, ending on 29 August, 1966 at Candlestick Park, San Francisco. Each of the four took cameras on stage to record the event, realising that their touring days were now over.

Opposite: 27 November, 1966. John makes a second guest appearance on Peter Cook and Dudley Moore's comedy show *Not Only ... But Also*. He played the commissionaire of a 'members only' club – a gents' lavatory. The scene was shot in Broadwick Street, central London.

PENNY LANE

*Left: I*n January 1967 the Beatles were adding the finishing touches to a new McCartney song, 'Penny Lane', having completed 'Strawberry Fields Forever'. Commercial sense said that either of these superb songs should have been the next Beatles single, with a B-side filler. Brian Epstein wanted a huge hit and opted to put out a double A-side instead. The idea backfired when Engelbert Humperdinck's 'Release Me' kept the Beatles off the top spot, their first 'failure' after 12 successive number ones.

Opposite: Jane Asher spent the early months of 1967 touring America with the Bristol Old Vic. Paul was busy formulating his ideas for the next Beatles project, an album in which the group members would assume alter egos in a fictitious band. Following the title track of *Sgt. Pepper's Lonely Hearts Club Band*, the rest of the album was envisaged as a show compered by the band leader. The idea wasn't fully followed through, but *Sgt. Pepper* is still widely regarded as the first concept album.

ALL YOU NEED IS LOVE

Opposite: On 25 June, 1967, the Beatles made history by playing to an audience of 400 million across five continents. It was part of the *Our World* broadcast, a BBC idea for a global event using satellite technology. The Beatles chose to perform John's 'All You Need Is Love', which was written just days before and captured the zeitgeist perfectly. With its famous opening bars from the 'Marseillaise' it also had an apposite international flavour. There was a stellar studio audience for the live performance, including Mick Jagger, Keith Richard, Eric Clapton and Graham Nash. This classic anthem of the 'summer of love' gave the Beatles their 13th UK number one.

Above: Unveiling *Sgt. Pepper* to the world. It was the fruits of more than 700 hours' work, rather more than their debut album *Please Please Me*, which was completed inside a day.

SGT. PEPPER

Paul and John congratulate each other on the tour de force that was *Sgt. Pepper*. George's 'Within You Without You' reflected his leanings towards Eastern religion, culture and music. His preoccupations meant that the concept of *Sgt. Pepper* didn't particularly fire his imagination. Ringo was more enthusiastic, although the complex orchestral arrangements left him with a lot of time on his hands, which he put to use by learning to play chess. Ringo was 'second on the bill' as Billy Shears, singing 'With A Little Help From My Friends'. He balked at the line 'Would you stand up and throw tomatoes at me', which was duly changed. The album topped the UK chart for six months following its release on 1 June, 1967. Even the gatefold sleeve and printed lyrics were ground-breaking. The Peter Blake-designed cover was conceived as a collection of the group's heroes. Sir Joseph Lockwood, the head of EMI, feared lawsuits from those portrayed who were still living and insisted that written consent be obtained. Almost all agreed, flattered to be on the cover of a prestigious new Beatles album.

SOUND EXPERIMENTS

Opposite: The Harrisons, Ringo and Alexis Mardas, whom the Beatles dubbed 'Magic Alex'. Mardas was an electronics wizard whose outlandish inventions appealed to the group – particularly John – at a time when they were experimenting with new sounds and ideas. In July 1967 Mardas accompanied the Beatles to Greece, where they planned to buy an island and establish a commune. It was a short-lived idea.

Right: John, with Julian. At one *Sgt. Pepper* studio session John felt unwell after taking LSD. Naively, George Martin led him up to the roof of the EMI building to get some fresh air. The rest of the group quickly rescued John, realising that only a small parapet had stood between him and a long drop to the street below. The album would be seen as an LSD-inspired work, particularly when fans noticed the acronym of 'Lucy in the Sky with Diamonds'. This was pure coincidence; the title came from a painting done by Julian.

A DAY IN THE LIFE

Left: Paul, Jane Asher and Julian Lennon. For the end of 'A Day In The Life' – *Sgt. Pepper's* grand finale – Paul conceived the idea of an orchestral build-up, each instrument proceeding from its lowest to its highest note in random time. John suggested that dogs ought not to be left out, and a high-pitched sound only audible to canines was added.

Opposite: Paul and John arrive home, following the Beatles' abortive attempt to buy a Greek island. One of the attractions had been to escape Britain's illiberal drug laws. There had been a media furore over Paul's recent admission that he had taken LSD. 'A Day In The Life' was banned by the BBC over concerns that it would promote drug use.

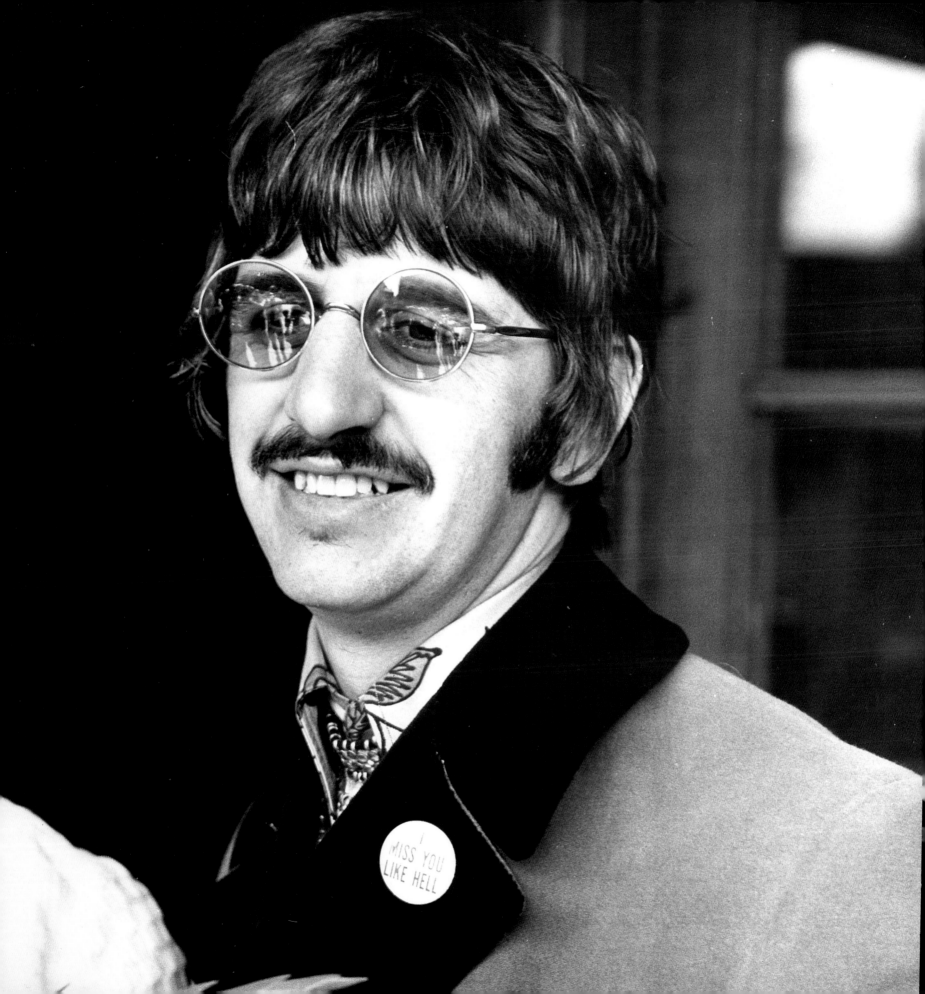

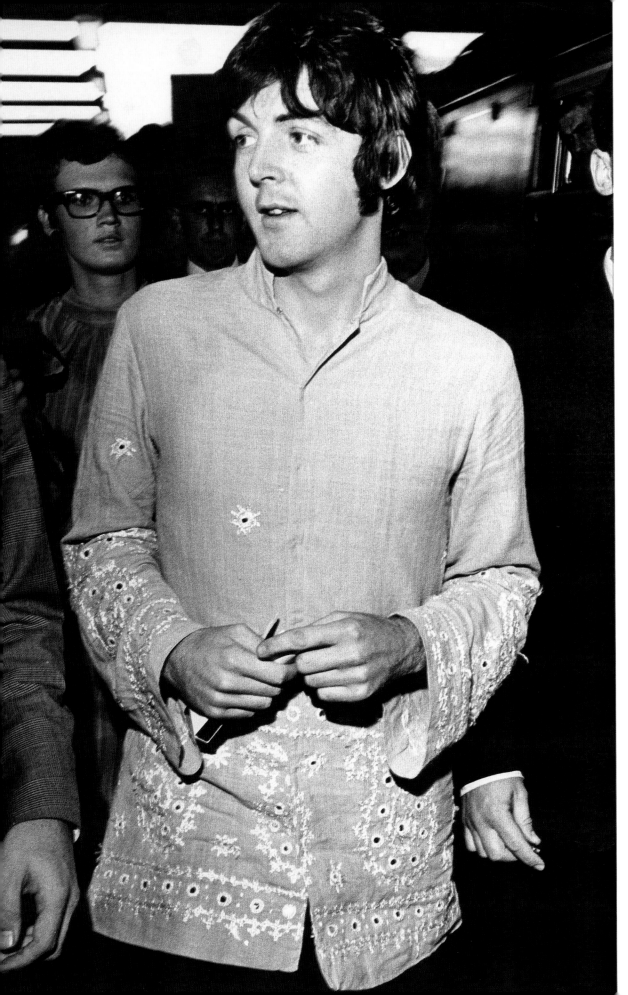

THE MAHARISHI

Opposite: 19 August, 1967. Ringo becomes a father for a second time when son Jason is born at Queen Charlotte's Hospital. Maureen's confinement meant that Ringo missed the lecture on transcendental meditation given by the Maharishi Mahesh Yogi at London's Hilton Hotel on 24 August. He joined the three other Beatles the following day when they travelled by train to Bangor for a weekend seminar hosted by the man they saw as their new guru.

Left: Paul at Euston Station, where the inevitable media scrum gets the weekend retreat in Bangor off to a frenetic start. The four needed all their spiritual reserves during their stay as news came through that Brian Epstein had been found dead. Since the touring had stopped there had been little for Epstein to do and the Beatles were increasingly taking control of their own affairs. He was prone to fits of depression and took all manner of pills. The verdict was death from an accidental overdose.

MAGICAL MYSTERY TOUR

September 1967. Paul pictured in Newquay during the filming of *Magical Mystery Tour*. As with *Sgt. Pepper*, Paul took the creative lead in the Beatles' latest project – a film based around a touring coach party. There was no script, just loose ideas for scenes and characters he wanted along for the ride. It was a patchy affair and predictably the musical set pieces were the high points, notably Paul's 'Fool on the Hill' and John's 'I Am the Walrus'. The latter, inspired by Lewis Carroll's work, was banned by the BBC for the 'knickers' reference in the lyrics.

John, during shooting in the West Country. When *Magical Mystery Tour* was shown on TV on 26 December, 1967 its running time was 52 minutes, some 10 hours of material having been left on the cutting-room floor. This made an eclectic concept appear even more disjointed and it was poorly received by viewers and critics alike. The fact that this kaleidoscope of ideas was shown in black and white didn't help, but it was still seen as the group's first major failure. Paul remarked: 'It wasn't the worst programme over Christmas. I mean, you couldn't call the Queen's Speech a gas either, could you?'

RINGO'S SOLO VENTURES

Left: Ringo and actress Eva Aulin, star of the film *Candy*. Ringo's performances in the Beatles films showed that he had a natural talent for acting and this was an obvious choice when it came to undertaking solo projects. In *Candy* Ringo played Emanuel, the Mexican gardener, a cameo role that required two weeks' filming in Rome in December 1967. The bawdy romp was panned by the critics but Ringo was unperturbed; he had appeared on the same film credits as Burton and Brando.

Opposite: 5 December, 1967. The Lennons and the Harrisons outside Apple Boutique, Baker Street, the Beatles' first commercial venture. They were reluctant businessmen, but were even more reluctant to let anyone else step into Epstein's shoes and exert control over them.

Chapter Five
1968-1969

Left: In late 1967 George joined the rest of the Beatles in adding a solo film project to his curriculum vitae. He was given *carte blanche* to write the score for the film *Wonderwall* and predictably he took the opportunity to indulge his passion for Indian music. In January 1968 he went to Bombay to record at the EMI studio there. The film was shown at Cannes in May and a soundtrack album, *Wonderwall Music*, was released on 1 November, the first LP to be put out on the Apple label.

Opposite: Brian Jones, Donovan and Cilla Black join the Beatles to launch new band Grapefruit, who would record under the fledgling Apple label. Grapefruit was a reincarnation of Tony Rivers and the Castaways, who had guested on the radio show *Pop Goes the Beatles* in 1963. The group had two Top 40 hits but would not set the pop world alight, or contribute much to the company coffers.

ENLIGHTENMENT IN INDIA

Paul and Jane Asher ended speculation by announcing their engagement on Christmas Day 1967. On 19 February, 1968, they flew to Rishikesh with Ringo and Maureen to study transcendental meditation under Maharishi Mahesh Yogi's tutelage. The Harrisons and Lennons had arrived in India four days earlier. The search for spiritual enlightenment was not a great success but it spawned some famous Beatles songs, many of which would feature on the famous *White Abum*. Paul wrote 'Ob-la-di Ob-la-da'; John penned 'Yer Blues' and 'The Continuing Story of Bungalow Bill'. He also composed 'Dear Prudence' as an exhortation to Mia Farrow's sister, who suffered from panic attacks and refused to come out of her chalet.

APPLE IS LAUNCHED

Opposite: In May 1968 John and Paul travelled to New York, a fitting place to announce the launch of Apple. The company's philosophy was to help others fulfil their dreams, as the Beatles themselves had done. Bottom-line profit would be a secondary issue.

Above: Paul gives his verdict on the five-week sojourn in India. His conclusion was that he could meditate in London as easily as Rishikesh, and he was now keen to return to the studio. All except George eventually lost faith in the Maharishi. There were allegations that the guru made improper advances towards one of the female guests, a charge which John set to music in the song 'Sexy Sadie'.

162

Left: Apple would have a number of offshoots but music remained the core business. James Taylor got his break on the new label, and Paul signed Mary Hopkin after seeing her performances on the TV talent show *Opportunity Knocks*. Even so, Apple's greatest asset was the songwriting talent of Lennon and McCartney.

Opposite: Even though Apple was all about giving artistic freedom to young talent it was still a corporate structure, which was anathema to a mind engrossed in Eastern mysticism. Much of the groundwork for the organisation was laid while George was still in India.

OUR FRIENDS ARE ALL ABOARD

Right: In His Own Write, a play based on John's two published books, opened at the Old Vic on 18 June, 1968. Its co-producer was Victor Spinetti, whose association with the Beatles went back to their first two films. 1968 saw the release of another Beatles film project, the animated feature *Yellow Submarine*, which received its premiere on 17 July. After an initial input the Beatles' interest in the project waned.

Opposite: Yoko Ono's arrival on the scene had a dramatically unsettling effect on the unique Beatles chemistry. Over the course of the year John and Yoko became inseparable, prompting Cynthia to file for divorce.

JOHN AND YOKO

Left: 1 July, 1968. John's first art exhibition was staged at the Robert Fraser Gallery in London. Entitled 'You Are Here', it consisted of a collection of charity boxes. Yoko Ono encouraged John to expand his artistic horizons, to apply the brilliant imagery of his lyrics to other media. The Beatles were working on a new album, but to John the group was not the only – perhaps not even the central – artistic outlet any longer.

Opposite: John with Julian and Yoko. Yoko Ono was still married to film director Anthony Cox when she and John met. The burgeoning relationship placed intolerable strains on the Beatles as she became a fixture during recording sessions. Ringo was the first to succumb to the pressures, walking out on the group in late August. He returned ten days later.

THE WHITE ALBUM

Left: In October 1968 John and Yoko were charged with cannabis possession. Close friend Brian Jones of the Rolling Stones paid the ultimate price for his drug habit the following year. Despite the growing tension within the group they produced yet another acclaimed album in 1968. The stark white cover of *The Beatles* was in complete contrast to *Sgt. Pepper* and gave the album its more colloquial name. George Martin suggested that the 30 songs be whittled down to produce a single LP. The group chose to keep the work intact and put out a double album. It was yet another triumph, although more the fruits of individual talents than of a coherent unit.

Opposite: Paul and Jane Asher's relationship finally ended in July 1968. He first met Linda Eastman at the Bag o' Nails, a regular haunt for the Beatles and some of their music business friends, including Georgie Fame and the Animals. Linda was on a photographic assignment, taking pictures of musicians for a book entitled *Rock and Other Four-Letter Words*.

GETTING BACK

At the end of 1968 Paul attempted to rekindle the Beatles flame by suggesting a return to live performance. The scheduled concerts failed to materialise but there was a commitment to return to the studio at the start of the new year, with cameras allowed in for a proposed documentary film. The project was provisionally entitled *Get Back*, an indication that Paul at least aspired to recreating the magic of the Beatles at their unified best.

Opposite: The beard was about to disappear, but not before the famous 42-minute concert on the roof of the Apple building on 30 January, 1969. Keyboard player Billy Preston joined the group for the set, which included 'Get Back' and 'Don't Let Me Down', the two sides of their next single. There was chaos in the streets below as hordes of fans looked skywards, and the police were eventually brought in to restore order.

Above: The photographer became the subject as Linda was seen out with Paul at a number of social functions. It was falsely reported in the press that she was part of the Eastman family whose name was synonymous with photographic equipment.

PAUL AND LINDA MARRY

On 12 March, 1969, speculation about Paul and Linda ended with an understated wedding ceremony. The couple married at Marylebone register office and later had the marriage blessed at St John's Wood parish church. Relations with the other Beatles were now at rock bottom. John spent the day at the recording studio. Apart from the charge that Paul was trying to run the group there was now a schism over their business dealings. John, George and Ringo wanted New York businessman Allen Klein to sort out Apple's chaotic affairs. Paul wanted to be represented by Eastman and Eastman, a company run by Linda's father and brother.

Paul broke millions of girls' hearts when he and Linda tied the knot. It was Linda, a divorcée
with a six-year-old daughter, Heather, who had to be persuaded to give marriage a second chance,
despite the fact that the groom was one of the world's most eligible bachelors.

DRUGS RAID

Left: While Paul and Linda were getting married the police were conducting a drugs raid on George and Pattie's Surrey home. They were later fined £250 each for cannabis possession. In January George had followed Ringo in becoming the second Beatle to walk out of the group. He too eventually returned, but stipulated that he was interested only in completing studio projects; all thoughts of live performance were off the agenda.

Opposite: Eight days after Paul and Linda's wedding John and Yoko married at the British Consulate in Gibraltar. Shortly afterwards John officially changed his middle name to Ono. Two bed-ins in the name of peace followed, the first at the Amsterdam Hilton, the second at the Queen Elizabeth Hotel in Montreal.

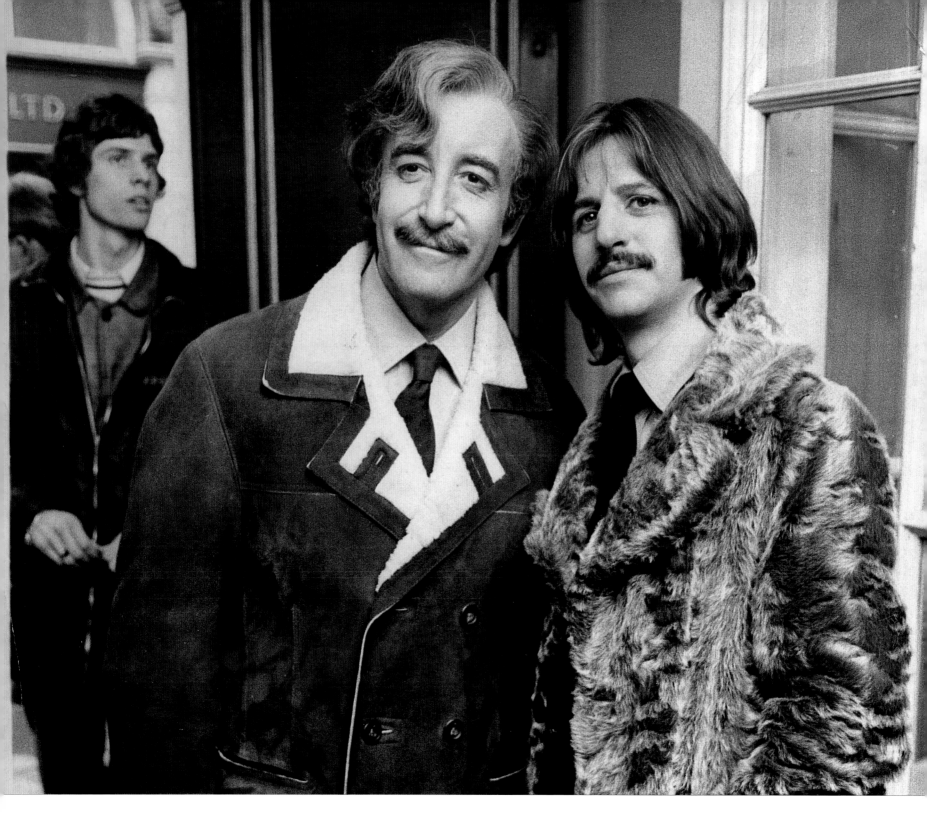

Above: Ringo spent the spring of 1969 filming *The Magic Christian*, which also starred Peter Sellers. After the unhappy studio sessions at the beginning of the year the Beatles put aside their differences for a glorious swansong. Ringo was even persuaded to do a drum solo on the *Abbey Road* track 'The End' something he had steadfastly refused to do until then.

Opposite: Five-year-old Kyoko Cox, Yoko's daughter from her first marriage, arrives from New York to meet her illustrious stepfather. By June 1969 John and Yoko had already released two avant-garde albums. Their new single, 'Give Peace A Chance', was a typical Lennon anthem which also had commercial appeal. It reached number two in June 1969, his first solo chart success.

ABBEY ROAD

Above: Linda was four months pregnant when she and Paul married. A daughter, Mary, was born on 28 August, 1969. Although *Abbey Road* was a triumphant last hurrah, the undercurrent of tension was still there. Paul, ever the perfectionist, spent three days simply getting his song 'Maxwell's Silver Hammer' the way he wanted it, something which irked the other band members.

Opposite: The Plastic Ono Band made its debut on 13 September, 1969, in Toronto, a rock 'n' roll revival which took John back to his first love. The fact that the new band was 'plastic' had significance: it would be pliable and flexible, the opposite of the straitjacket he felt the Beatles had become. The group included the new Lennon composition 'Cold Turkey' in the set which John had tendered as a possible Beatles single. That failed to materialise and it was recorded by the Plastic Ono Band. It was one of the final acts before the divorce was finalised.

SOMETHING IN THE WAY SHE MOVES

Left: John was in a minority when he described *Abbey Road* as 'a competent album; I don't think it is anything more than that or anything less'. The four were already mentally attuned to solo projects and in the final collaboration they were only really interested in their own contributions.

Opposite: George, with members of the Radha Krishna Temple, with whom he has the unlikeliest hit single of the year. 'The Hare Krishna Mantra' reached number 12 in the UK in September 1969. The following month 'Something' became the first Harrison-penned Beatles single. Many considered it the highlight of *Abbey Road*. As a songwriter George finally emerged from the shadows of Lennon and McCartney at the very moment when the Beatles were in terminal decline.

CAMPAIGNERS

December 1969. John and Yoko take up the cause of James Hanratty, convicted and hanged for the infamous A6 murder in 1962. John, who had just returned his MBE to Buckingham Palace, planned to make a film about what he believed to be a travesty of justice.

ALL WE ARE SAYING...

Left: The Lennons were tireless crusaders for world peace. In November 1969, 200,000 Americans demonstrated against the war in Vietnam by singing 'Give Peace A Chance' outside the White House. Renowned anthropologist Desmond Morris regarded Lennon's influence as of such magnitude that he nominated him Man of the Decade in a TV special to award that title.

Opposite: 15 December, 1969. The Plastic Ono Band on stage at the Lyceum Ballroom, London. John agreed to play the concert, for UNICEF, at short notice and co-opted a number of guests to join the line-up. These included Eric Clapton, Keith Moon – and George Harrison – the first appearance of two Beatles together on a British stage for over three years.

Chapter Six
1970-1971

Before the rift became terminal, Paul had wanted the Beatles to return to their roots. He was against Phil Spector who had been brought in to produce 'Let It Be'. The man famous for the 'wall of sound' was criticised by both McCartney and George Martin for over-production. In particular Paul hated Spector's orchestral arrangement on 'The Long and Winding Road'.

George, with virtuoso sitar player Ravi Shankar, at the Indian Arts season held at the Royal Albert Hall in September 1970. In November George released the acclaimed triple album, *All Things Must Pass*. In different circumstances the title song could easily have been yet another Harrison triumph on a Beatles album. The single 'My Sweet Lord', released in the UK early the following year, landed Harrison with another court action, this time over claims that he had plagiarised the Chiffons' hit 'He's So Fine'.

Left: In March 1970 Ringo completed his debut solo album, *Sentimental Journey*, a collection of old favourites with new arrangements. George Martin produced the album but there was no contribution from the other Beatles.

Opposite: When the Beatles finally disintegrated Paul and Linda spent a lot of time on their farm in Scotland. The creative urge soon took hold, and Paul started work on a solo album of his own, recorded on a four-track machine. He then worked on the album at Morgan Studios in Willesden under the name Billy Martin to keep the project under wraps.

Old habits die hard. John said he allowed the writing credit for 'Give Peace A Chance' to go to Lennon-McCartney, whereas it should have been ascribed to himself and Yoko. The days of joint-credit, even if one of them had done most of the work, were well and truly over.

The McCartneys en route to the St Tropez wedding of Mick Jagger and Bianca Perez-Mora. The Rolling Stones had been clients of Alan Klein's before his involvement with the Beatles. Their relationship had soured and Jagger tried to warn the Beatles about becoming involved with the New Yorker, but to no avail.

CONTRACTED TO EMI

Opposite: John was not smiling when he learned that the Beatles were bound to EMI – and thus to each other – for ten years. The band had always had a laissez faire attitude to contractual matters and were unaware of the legal situation. The contract was due to expire on 26 January, 1976.

Left: The Starrs were also guests at Jagger's wedding, giving the opportunity to thaw relations between Ringo and Paul. When Ringo called to see Paul to discuss the problem over the release of his and Paul's solo albums and 'Let It Be', Paul unceremoniously threw him out.

WINGS LINE-UP

Paul and Linda at the launch of Paul's new band. Wings' line-up was completed by Denny Seiwell *(left)*, who had played drums on McCartney's second album, *Ram*, and ex-Moody Blues singer Denny Laine. McCartney and Laine had known each other for years. Paul thought their voices complemented each other and 'Go Now', one of the Moody Blues' biggest hits, was a great favourite of Linda's. Their association would last ten years, longer than the lifespan of the Beatles, and also end acrimoniously.

Chapter Seven
1972-2004

Opposite: May 1972. The Harrisons and Starrs on their way to the Cannes Film Festival, where George's *Concert For Bangla Desh* is being shown.

Above: Paul had wanted the Beatles to recapture the spirit of the early days. He did just that with Wings by playing the university campus circuit, often turning up unannounced. Students paid fifty pence for the privilege of seeing McCartney's attempt to recreate the magic of the Cavern era.

RAM

Opposite: Wings' debut single was 'Give Ireland Back To The Irish', released February 1972. Written in response to the events of Bloody Sunday, it was a rare excursion for Paul into the realms of the political protest song, which until then had been John's domain. The BBC banned the record, the critics were lukewarm and it only reached number 13 in the UK chart.

Right: Linda was accorded joint writing credit for the album *Ram*. This deprived Lew Grade – who now owned Northern Songs – of 50 per cent of the royalties. The case went to court to test whether Linda had the musical competence to justify the credit she received. The McCartneys won the case.

RINGO'S A STAR

Right: 1973 was a productive year for Ringo. As well as enhancing his acting reputation with his performance in *That'll Be The Day*, he had two hit singles, 'Photograph' and 'You're Sixteen'. His second album, *Ringo*, released at the end of the year was also a Top 10 hit.

Opposite: Paul and Linda's second daughter, Stella Nina, was born 13 September, 1971. Here, two-year-old Stella donates one of her teddies to a charity in aid of sick children.

LIVE AND LET DIE

Opposite: Proud parents first, rock stars second. Linda continued to attract criticism for her musical ability. Denny Laine thought the group would have scaled the heights more quickly with a superior keyboard player. Linda herself reached the point where she wanted to leave the group.

Right: In May 1973 Wings embarked on their first proper British tour. The second album, *Red Rose Speedway*, was better received, as was Paul's theme song for the new Bond movie, *Live And Let Die*. For both he renewed his partnership with George Martin.

After early successes George's career stalled in the mid-1970s. He formed the Dark Horse label in 1974, released an album of the same title and went on tour in America. It was too far removed from Beatles' music for the fans' liking.

BAND ON THE RUN

Paul and Linda on the road with the children. In the summer of 1973 Wings – now just the McCartneys
and Denny Laine – went to Lagos, Nigeria, to record *Band on the Run*. It gave the group their first
number one album, while the assembly of stars on the sleeve was reminiscent of *Sgt. Pepper*.

235

Opposite: *Walls and Bridges*, *Rock and Roll*, and *Shaved Fish* gave John three Top 10 albums within a year in 1974-5. None matched the success of *Band on the Run*, about which John was highly complimentary. During this period he separated temporarily from Yoko Ono but there was a reconciliation in January 1975. Sean Ono Lennon was born on 9 October that year and John announced that he was taking an extended sabbatical to enjoy fatherhood second time round.

Above: Wings in concert at the Empire Pool, Wembley. 'Picasso's Last Words', on the *Band on the Run* album, was written to order from a newspaper article. Actor Dustin Hoffmann showed McCartney the random clipping and was stunned to find that the superstar really could compose on the spot. The album's title track and 'Jet' were both hit singles for Wings in 1974.

Paul and Linda on stage during one of two Wings concerts in which they played to 8,000 people at the Empire Pool, Wembley.

LONDON TOWN

Above: Paul, Linda and Denny Laine take a boat ride down the Thames, and feast on fish and chips, to promote Wings' new album *London Town*.

Opposite: By 1978 George was looking more relaxed, having finally sorted out his divorce from Pattie. He was also starting anew in several fields – new love with Olivia Arias, later to become his wife; a new interest, Grand Prix racing; and renewed musical success with critical acclaim for his most recent album, *33¹/₃*.

McCARTNEY STYLE

Left: Despite touring and charity commitments Paul and Linda took care to spend as much time as possible with their children: Heather, Linda's daughter from her first marriage, Stella, Mary and James. Paul and Linda, pictured here with Heather and Stella, are wearing stylish hats.

Opposite: Relaxing after a concert at the Hammersmith Odeon given in aid of UNICEF and Kampuchean refugees. Wings and a collection of Paul's 'Rochestra' musicians had played at the end of a week-long series of concerts.

RINGO MARRIES AGAIN

Opposite: In April 1981 Ringo marries actress Barbara Bach in London. It was just four months since John had been gunned down by a crazed fan, outside his New York apartment, on 8 December 1980 and Ringo's wedding was a chance for the remaining Beatles to meet on a more celebratory occasion.

Left: Thumbs up from Paul as he is photographed on the gate of his Sussex farm following eight days' imprisonment and deportation from Japan, after a large amount of cannabis was found stashed in his luggage.

GIVE MY REGARDS TO BROAD STREET

Above: At the Hippodrome, Paul strikes a pose against a backdrop of Linda, Olivia, Barbara and Ringo before the London première of his film *Give My Regards to Broad Street*. Ringo and Barbara starred in the film, along with Paul and Linda. Ringo was taking on an increasing number of film roles and also won acclaim in the eighties as the voice of the *Thomas the Tank Engine* series.

Opposite: Always ready to fool around for the cameras, Paul jives to the jukebox at his Soho office.

GEORGE ON SONG

Opposite: At a concert in honour of rock'n'roll singer Carl Perkins, George shows he still enjoys his music.

Left: George on the set of *Shanghai Surprise,* the latest of his HandMade Films projects. HandMade was enjoying great critical and box office success – in 1986, the year *Shanghai Surprise* premièred, *My Beautiful Laundrette* was honoured as Best British Picture of the Year at the *Evening Standard* awards ceremony, while *A Private Function* won the award for Best Screen Play and its star Michael Palin took the Peter Sellers Comedy Award.

HAPPY BIRTHDAY SGT. PEPPER!

Opposite: Flanked by Linda and Peter Blake, the artist responsible for the album cover, Paul cuts a massive cake at a party to celebrate 20 years since the release of *Sgt. Pepper's Lonely Hearts Club Band* in June 1967.

Above: Always willing to use his music to help others, George played alongside bands such as the Moody Blues and The Electric Light Orchestra at Heartbeat '86 in Birmingham's NEC, to raise money for a local children's hospital.

ON THE ROAD AGAIN

Above: Paul on stage at the end of the eighties with a new band specially formed to back him during a twelve-month tour that he dedicated to Friends of the Earth. Although the pressure group did not receive any profits from the tour, there was an opportunity to promote their views in the programme.

George plays guitar with Eric Clapton and Elton John in the Prince's Trust Rock Concert in 1987. Ten years later he was diagnosed with cancer and a tumour was removed from his neck; the cancer returned and on 29 November, 2001, aged 58, George died. Up until his death, music continued to play an important role in his life, despite success as a film producer. In the late eighties he formed the Travelling Wilburys with Bob Dylan, Tom Petty, Roy Orbison and Jeff Lynne and just before his death he revealed he had been working on a new album, Brainwashed, which was released in 2002.

BACK IN THE WORLD

Above: After the tragedy of Linda's death from breast cancer in 1998, Paul met former model Heather Mills through her charity work. The couple married in 2002 and in October 2003, Heather gave birth to a daughter, Beatrice. Heather encouraged Paul to tour again and the Back in the World tour of 2002/2003 was a triumphant success.

Opposite: When *Q* magazine published its 100 Greatest Stars of the twentieth century, Paul came in at number two with Ringo, who continued to tour with his All Starrs Band, at number 26 and George at number 36 but the winner in the poll, voted for by readers, was John Lennon.

'The Beatles were always a great band. Nothing more, nothing less.'

Paul McCartney